MILITARY SPECIAL OPS

ARMY
DELTA FORCE

ELITE OPERATIONS

BY MARCIA AMIDON LUSTED

Lerner Publications Company
Minneapolis

Lerner Publications Company
A division of Lerner Publishing Group, Inc.
241 First Avenue North
Minneapolis, MN 55401 U.S.A.

Website address: www.lernerbooks.com

Content Consultant: Kalev Sepp, assistant professor, Naval Postgraduate
School

Library of Congress Cataloging-in-Publication Data

Lusted, Marcia Amidon.
    Army Delta Force : elite operations / by Marcia Amidon Lusted.
        pages   cm. — (Military special ops)
    Includes index.
    ISBN 978-0-7613-9077-0 (lib. bdg. : alk. paper)
    ISBN 978-1-4677-1762-5 (eBook)
    1. United States. Army. Delta Force—Juvenile literature. 2. United
States. Army—Commando troops—Juvenile literature. I. Title.
UA34.S64L87 2014
356'.167—dc23   2013001736

Manufactured in the United States of America
1 — MG — 7/15/13

The images in this book are used with the permission of: © Aleksandar
Mijatovic/Shutterstock Images, backgrounds; © Kevin Frayer/AP Images,
5; © David Guttenfelder/AP Images, 7; © Laurent Rebours/AP Images,
8; U.S. Army Special Operations Command, 9, 21; U.S. Army, 11, 20;
© AP Images, 11; © Captain Keating/IWM/Getty Images, 12–13;
Bradley C. Church/U.S. Department of Defense, 14; © Mai/Time Life
Pictures/Getty Images, 15; Dean D. Wagner/U.S. Department of Defense,
17; Trish Harris/U.S. Army, 18; Jeremy D. Crisp/Special Operations
Task Force South, 22; Jonathan Lovelady/U.S. Air Force, 25, 27; Tony R.
Ritter/U.S. Air Force, 26; Tony Hawkins/U.S. Army Special Operations
Command, 28; U.S. Department of Defense, 29.

Front cover: U.S. Army Photo by Sgt. David William McLean, 22nd MPAD.

Main body text set in Tw Cen MT Std Medium 12/18.
Typeface provided by Adobe Systems.

CONTENTS

CHAPTER ONE: GET BIN LADEN

They were given one order from the Pentagon: kill or capture Osama bin Laden. It was only ten weeks after the September 11, 2001, terrorist attacks on the United States. The U.S. government turned to one of its most elite, secret special operations teams. Special Forces Operational Detachment Delta—known as Delta Force—was given the mission. Get bin Laden, the mastermind behind the attacks.

The Central Intelligence Agency (CIA) knew bin Laden was hiding in the Afghanistan mountains. Delta Force operators flew from their base in North Carolina to Afghanistan. Local Afghan fighters joined them there. Together they all piled into pickup trucks.

KEEPING SECRETS

Delta Force relies on secrecy to help accomplish their missions. They often can't look like ordinary soldiers. That would alert enemies they were coming. The aircraft in which they travel are painted and outfitted to look like civilian aircraft. The team members often wear civilian clothing. Disguises are especially important when the U.S. government or military must hide its mission.

Afghan allies of the United States ride in a pickup truck near Tora Bora, Afghanistan, in 2001.

Interviewer: "The idea is that if this all worked out . . . no one would ever know that Delta Force was there?"

Dalton Fury, Delta Force team commander: "That's the plan. And that always is when you're talking about Delta Force."

—Interview, CBS's 60 Minutes

They traveled to a place high in the mountains called Tora Bora. It was a very difficult place to stage an attack. They would have to fight men from al-Qaeda, bin Laden's terrorist group. To get close to their objective, the operators disguised themselves as Afghan soldiers. The operators wore Afghan clothing, carried Afghan weapons, and let their beards grow out.

In the mountains, they fought with al-Qaeda for four days. Several Delta Force operators became trapped behind enemy lines. The rest of the team rescued their teammates. Then they drew near the hilltop where bin Laden was said to be hiding. The operators saw a cave they hadn't seen before. Fifty enemy men were moving into the cave. One of the men was tall and wearing a camouflage jacket. The team knew bin Laden was well over 6 feet (1.8 meters) tall. They thought the man could be their target.

This was their chance. The Delta Force operators ordered U.S. planes to drop bombs on the cave. All the men inside were killed. The explosions sealed the caves shut. The team believed they killed the terrorist mastermind that day. Later, they opened up the collapsed cave. They examined each of the enemy bodies hoping to identify bin Laden. But they were not so lucky. Eventually bin Laden released a video of himself. He had not been in the caves during the attack after all. He had most likely been wounded earlier and taken to a safe place.

Afghan forces watch U.S. planes bomb Tora Bora.

Saddam Hussein hid in this tiny hole in the ground near Tikrit, Iraq.

MISSION IN FOCUS

SADDAM HUSSEIN

One of Delta Force's most famous missions took place in 2003. They found and captured Saddam Hussein. He was the ruler of Iraq. In the past, he had started two wars with his neighbors, Iran and Kuwait. Countries including the United States accused him of preparing to start another war by building long-range rockets. The United States and several allied nations sent troops to attack Saddam's forces in Iraq. The troops destroyed the rockets and seized Saddam's palace. However, the dictator had already escaped. Intelligence discovered that Saddam was hiding at a farm near Tikrit, Iraq. Delta Force operators worked with U.S. Army Special Forces and other soldiers. They surrounded the farm. They found Saddam in a small underground hideout. Delta Force used their training in handling angry prisoners. They subdued Saddam and put him in handcuffs with a bag over his head. Then they put him in a helicopter. They flew him to a secret location as quickly as possible. Delta Force was worried Saddam's followers might try to rescue him. They guarded him around the clock. Saddam was tried in court by the new Iraqi government in 2004. The court found him guilty of killing thousands of his fellow Iraqis. He was put to death for his crimes in 2006.

Another U.S. special operations force, the U.S. Navy SEALs, killed bin Laden in 2011. But the Delta Force special mission unit continues to be one of the United States' greatest weapons against terrorism. The unit is secretive. Its membership and activities are highly classified. Its members come from every branch of the military. Only a small group of government officials knows for sure how many soldiers belong to the unit. Members of the group are expert snipers and close-quarters combatants. They know how to enter and leave an area without being seen. They use all types of explosives. At a moment's notice, they can be sent anywhere in the world to defend their country . . . even though they don't officially exist.

All Delta Force operators receive sniper training.

CHAPTER TWO: DELTA FORCE IS BORN

Delta Force was the first counterterrorism unit in the U.S. military. It is also one of the most secret. It even has several different names. It is called Special Forces Operational Detachment Delta, the Combat Applications Group (CAG), or the Army Compartmented Element (ACE). Most Delta Force members just call their group the Unit.

Delta Force was formed because of increasing terrorist activity in the 1970s. Terrorist activities such as bombings and hijackings were taking place more often. The United States needed a special group to deal with this kind of trouble. Colonel Charles Beckwith of the U.S. Army

COLONEL BECKWITH

Charles Beckwith was born in Georgia in 1929. He played football at the University of Georgia. He joined the U.S. Army after graduation. He volunteered for the new Army Special Forces when it formed. He served heroically during the Vietnam War (1957–1975). Afterward, he built up his new counterterrorism unit at Fort Bragg in North Carolina. However, the group's first major mission, to rescue hostages in Iran, was unsuccessful. Beckwith retired from the army soon after. He died in 1994.

Incidents such as this 1971 bombing in Ireland convinced the U.S. government that terrorism was a growing threat.

had an idea. He began envisioning a U.S. counterterrorist force in the 1960s. He first got the idea after spending time with the British Special Air Service (SAS) in 1962. The SAS was a carefully chosen group of British soldiers. They could respond quickly to terrorist activities. The SAS also operated secretly.

Colonel Charles Beckwith

During World War II (1939–1945), the British SAS wore the protective headdress of the local people in North Africa.

Beckwith thought the U.S. Army needed this kind of counterterrorist group. It took the rise in terrorism for the army to seriously consider his idea, which had been ignored for years. He finally received permission to create Delta Force in 1977. He recruited men from all branches of the army. He chose many who had recently fought in the Vietnam War. They would be the best-trained force in the U.S. military. They would be part of the army. However, they could be assigned to help whoever needed them. This might mean the army, the Federal Bureau of Investigation (FBI), or the CIA. And Delta Force was a secret group. The U.S. government would not publicly admit they existed.

Today, Delta Force is not entirely secret. Public government documents refer to the unit. Its commanders and heroes receive public awards. But the government says as little as possible about the unit. It is hard to find trustworthy information about Delta Force and what it does. There are very few official reports.

"Speed, surprise, and violence of action."
— Delta Force unofficial motto, quoted in Robin Moore's The Hunt for Bin Laden: Task Force Dagger

Communication is critical for Delta Force teams.

Delta Force is organized very similarly to the British SAS. The U.S. group operates out of Fort Bragg, North Carolina. Delta Force is divided into three squadrons: A, B, and C. Each squadron is made up of three troops. This includes one troop of snipers and two troops of assault soldiers. A troop includes four to five groups of four to five men each, or sixteen to twenty-five men total. The two assault troops specialize in air, ground, or water attacks. The troops can also be broken up into smaller teams with as many as twelve men or as few as one man.

Delta Force also has several support units. An aviation unit flies them to their targets in helicopters. Delta Force also has a general support unit and a signals unit. These groups include medical staff, logistics experts, and signalers who specialize in radio communication. There is also a unit of soldiers who gather intelligence, similar to spies.

Delta Force is different from regular military forces in several ways. Operators do not always dress like regular soldiers. The sergeants and officers do not treat one another as formally as they do in much of the rest of the military. They also use new and unusual kinds of equipment.

Delta Force is one of the most elite and secret groups in the U.S. Army Special Forces. Secrecy helps them carry out counterterrorism, which is their most important mission.

Delta Force headquarters is located at Fort Bragg in North Carolina.

CHAPTER THREE:
BLENDING IN

From the start, Delta Force was meant to fight terrorists. This is the unit's most important role. It involves many different types of missions. Operators might rescue hostages in a foreign country. They might capture a terrorist leader. They even act as bodyguards for U.S. military officials in dangerous places. They guarded General Norman Schwarzkopf in Iraq in 1991. Recently, they guarded Afghan president Hamid Karzai.

RUMORS

The U.S. government keeps Delta Force missions as secret as possible. Sometimes when special forces units from other countries carry out missions, rumors say Delta Force was also involved. For example, an Indonesian Airlines flight was hijacked in 1981. Indonesian special forces saved the hostages. But some say Delta Force was involved. The U.S. government does not confirm or deny this.

A Delta Force operator dressed in street clothes guards General Schwarzkopf, *left.*

Delta Force members can go deep into enemy territory. They can find hidden weapons such as missiles. They place targets so other U.S. military forces can destroy these weapons. Delta Force soldiers can operate aircraft, trains, ships, and other kinds of vehicles. They can take control of these vehicles in any situation. This prepares Delta Force to rescue hijacked airplanes.

The Night Stalkers are helicopter specialists.

MISSION IN FOCUS

BLACK HAWK DOWN

Delta Force carried out a mission on October 3, 1993. The mission was portrayed in the movie *Black Hawk Down*. Operators arrived in Mogadishu, the capital of Somalia, in eastern Africa. They attempted to capture the Somali warlord Aidid. Delta Force soldiers roped down from helicopters into a slum. Aidid's men were meeting there. U.S. Army Rangers drove through the streets in trucks. They would evacuate the Delta soldiers and their prisoners. However, one of the U.S. helicopters was shot down. There were now wounded pilots and Delta Force operators trapped on the ground. Armed Somali gangs surrounded them. These gangs fired on the U.S. soldiers. Finally, two other Delta Force members volunteered to help the trapped soldiers. They dropped by ropes from a helicopter. The Delta Force operators rallied the troops and helped them fight their way out. Both Delta Force volunteers were killed. The two men, Master Sergeant Gary Gordon and Sergeant First Class Randall Shughart, received the Medal of Honor. The Medal of Honor is a high honor. These were the first medals awarded since the Vietnam War.

Delta Force soldiers might watch training camps for terrorists and antigovernment rebels. They set up sophisticated surveillance equipment. They have helped U.S.-friendly countries like Chad. They trained the Chad military in the use of high-tech weapons. Above all, Delta Force squadrons must be ready to go into action at any moment, day or night.

Sometimes Delta Force operators call in a special unit of pilots. The 160th Special Operations Aviation Regiment is also known as the Night Stalkers. This army unit supports Delta Force. The Night Stalker pilots fly helicopters very close to the ground. They deliver Delta Force operators secretly. The Night Stalkers use special equipment such as night-vision goggles to fly at night. They use helicopters without lights so they will not be seen. They claim they can arrive at any destination anywhere within thirty seconds of their goal time.

But it takes more than training and special skills for Delta Force to accomplish its missions. They need the best equipment available.

CHAPTER FOUR: AT A MOMENT'S NOTICE

Delta Force soldiers need many different types of equipment to carry out their missions. Some of the most important gear is their weapons.

Delta Force has access to the best weapons in the world. And the Delta operators usually customize them to work even better. Delta Force has its own gunsmiths. They adjust the grips, sights, stocks, and moving parts of standard weapons. This makes each weapon fit the exact needs of each operator. The gunsmiths also make their own ammunition. This makes the guns more reliable.

Delta Force operators commonly carry M4 assault rifles.

This sniper's gear allows him to blend in almost perfectly with his surroundings.

Delta Force soldiers carry several types of weapons. M4 assault rifles and sidearms are personalized to fit each man exactly. Soldiers might also use machine guns, shotguns, submachine guns, and sniper rifles. Gun manufacturers work directly with Delta Force to develop special weapons just for the operators.

Night-vision goggles can be crucial for Delta Force missions.

Delta Force operators going into the field take very specific equipment. They often wear a custom-made vest or belt. Their pockets and belt clips hold grenades, ammunition, tourniquets, knives, a GPS device, batteries, tools, and explosive charges. One operator described his gear as a real-life version of Batman's utility belt. The operators also carry medical kits. They wear helmets with flip-down night-vision goggles, ear protection, and radios for communicating with one another.

THE RIGHT HAIR FOR THE JOB

After the terrorist attacks on the United States on September 11, 2001, many Delta Force soldiers immediately stopped shaving. They knew they might need to go to Afghanistan in a hurry. Men in Afghanistan generally have long beards. The Delta Force men needed to be able to work among the locals without looking out of place, so they also grew beards.

Unlike most regular military units, Delta Force does not have just one uniform. Many missions require that Delta Force operators do not look like military personnel. They go anywhere in the world and must blend in with any population. They do not have traditional short military haircuts. They often wear civilian clothing. Delta Force members usually do not wear patches that show their unit. Sometimes they wear a small U.S. flag attached with Velcro. They can remove the flag patch if they have to.

Even with its special equipment, however, Delta Force is only as good as its operators. And that takes training.

"In Delta Force, the uniform standard is largely personal choice. As long as an operator can do his job on target—slide down a rope from a hovering helicopter, enter the breach, eliminate the threat efficiently, and dominate the room—why should I care [what he wears]?"

—Dalton Fury, author of *Kill Bin Laden*

CHAPTER FIVE: HOUSE OF HORRORS

Delta Force soldiers are among the most highly trained special forces soldiers in the world. Training is difficult. Only the strongest and smartest men make it into this special unit. They are carefully chosen during a selection process.

Delta Force candidates usually come from the U.S. Army Special Forces or from the U.S. Army Rangers. However, anyone in the U.S. Army can volunteer to join. Selection takes a month. The process

FITNESS TESTS

Recruits must score high on the U.S. Army's physical fitness tests to qualify for Delta Force training. Minimum qualifying scores are these:

★ Fifty-five push-ups in two minutes

★ Sixty-two sit-ups in two minutes

★ A 2-mile (3.2-kilometer) run in 15:06 or less

However, recruits must get stronger and faster quickly to complete their training.

Delta Force training includes nighttime actions under challenging conditions.

happens twice a year. Recruits must pass a physical exam, a security check, and a physical fitness test. Then they go through even harder tests. This includes a nighttime 18-mile (29 km) speed walk carrying a 35-pound (16-kilogram) rucksack. Next comes a 40-mile (64 km) endurance march. The recruits are given a spot on a map to reach as quickly as possible. They carry a 45-pound (20 kg) rucksack. The terrain is difficult. At each spot, they get a new map and a new place to reach. This goes on for as long as twelve or fourteen hours. They are given new places to find each time. Usually darkness falls, and the spots become more difficult to reach.

Delta Force operators must be able to fast-rope from helicopters.

The recruits who make it through must pass a series of psychological and mental evaluations. This tests what kind of person each one is. The experts making these evaluations decide if the volunteers will function well in Delta Force. At the end of these tests, only about 10 percent of the original volunteers are left.

Those who pass move on to a five-month training program called the Operators Training Course. Much of their training takes place at the Delta Force compound at Fort Bragg. Details about the compound are kept secret. It is said to include an Olympic-size swimming pool, several firing ranges, a three-story climbing wall, and a deep tank for scuba diving. The climbing wall is important. Delta Force members must be able to climb up buildings and mountain cliffs. They also need to be able to fast-rope from helicopters.

Trainees must learn to rescue hostages and enter enemy locations. They use an indoor training facility nicknamed the House of Horrors. This is set up to simulate a house where hostages need to be rescued. The Delta Force trainees might find themselves in simulated gunfire or surrounded with choking smoke. In another simultion, they might have to stop an airplane hijacking.

Special forces soldiers practice interrogating a person of interest during a training exercise.

Delta Force operators must develop their shooting skills.

The House of Horrors has sophisticated simulation systems that can be easily changed. One room has a projection system. It might project a video of a room filled with hostages and terrorists. Trainees must decide which people are the terrorists and which people are the hostages. They must not shoot anyone they are trying to rescue. The operators can pause the video to see which people have been hit. Other rooms have plastic silhouettes of people that pop up as shooting targets. Trainees must shoot only the bad guys.

Mastery of weapons is crucial in Delta Force. Soldiers have to train in shooting. They might train for hours every day. They should hit 100 percent of their targets with their rifles from a distance of 600 yards (550 m). They must also hit 90 percent of their targets when they shoot their rifles from 1,000 yards (910 m).

Delta Force trainees practice these and other skills over and over again. They must learn to perform without any mistakes. They learn to work surrounded by smoke, gunshots, and explosions. In the end, they will become part of one of the most skilled counterterrorist units in the world. They can perform their missions secretly and not be seen or identified. As terrorism continues to be a problem in the twenty-first century, Delta Force has the men, training, and equipment to protect the United States.

Few verifiable images of Delta Force operators are released by the government. Many of these images cover the operators' faces to maintain secrecy.

GLOSSARY

AL-QAEDA
violent terrorist organization responsible for the September 11, 2001, attacks in the United States

ASSAULT
military attack on enemy forces

CAMOUFLAGE
disguising military equipment or people by covering or painting them so they blend in with their surroundings

CIVILIAN
person not serving in the military

COUNTERTERRORISM
political or military activities designed to stop terrorism

EVACUATE
to move someone from a dangerous place to a safe one

FAST-ROPE
technique used to slide down a rope from a helicopter

INTELLIGENCE
information of military or political value

LOGISTICS
the selection, buying, repair, and transportation of military supplies

SURVEILLANCE
keeping a close watch on something

TERRAIN
the physical features of a piece of land

LEARN MORE

Further Reading

Alvarez, Carlos. *Army Delta Force*. Minneapolis: Bellwether Media, 2009.

Labrecque, Ellen. *Heroic Jobs: Special Forces*. Chicago: Heinemann-Raintree, 2012.

Lusted, Marcia Amidon. *Army Rangers: Elite Operations*. Minneapolis: Lerner Publications Company, 2014.

Nagle, Jeanne. *US Special Forces: Delta Force*. New York: Gareth Stevens Publishing, 2012.

Websites

American Special Ops.com

http://deltaforce.americanspecialops.com/

This website tells all about Delta Force and its operations, equipment, and training.

How Stuff Works: How Delta Force Works

http://science.howstuffworks.com/delta-force.htm

This website features an overview of Delta Force, including how it works and some of its missions.

United States Army

http://www.goarmy.com/special-forces.html

The official army website includes links to U.S. Army Special Forces information.

About the Author

Marcia Amidon Lusted has written more than seventy-five books for young readers. She is also a magazine editor, a writing instructor, and a musician.